A Dog and His Duck

A Very UNLIKELY PAIR

Shelley Jukanovich

ISBN 978-1-64492-855-4 (paperback)
ISBN 978-1-64416-174-6 (hardcover)
ISBN 978-1-64416-173-9 (digital)

Christian Faith Publishing, Inc.
832 Park Avenue
Meadville, PA 16335
www.christianfaithpublishing.com

Printed in the United States of America

In Memory of Bo Bear & Duck Duck

A dog and a duck
A very unlikely pair
Whose odd friendship
Made people stop and stare

Bo Bear was a big boy
His color black and white
140 pounds of muscle—
He was quite a sight

Duck Duck was a mallard duck
His color black and green
Just three pounds of skin and feathers
He was a brave little thing

Bo Bear was a gentle giant
Unaware of his own strength
Duck Duck was his best friend
With whom he played at length

Back and forth they would tease
Playing for hours and hours

Bo Bear biting Duck Duck's tail
Duck Duck hanging from Bo's jowls

Chasing was a daily game
From one end of the yard to the other
This way then that way they ran and waddled
Teasing each other like brothers

Swimming in the beaver pond
Became their favorite game
Around and around they would go
Bo ignoring the sound of his name

Bo Bear chasing Duck Duck
Panting as he swam along
Duck Duck making secret plans
As the Marsh Wrens broke into song

Silently, Duck Duck would dive under the water
Popping up behind his friend

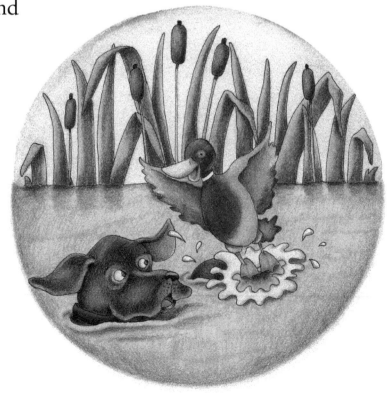

Then he would hop on Bo Bear's back
And they would do it all over again

After a while when the sun was setting
And the dog and the duck would tire
They would make their way through the cattail
marshes—drawn by the light of a glowing fire.

As the people gathered around the fire
Talking quietly about their day
Bo Bear and Duck Duck
Would fall asleep on some hay

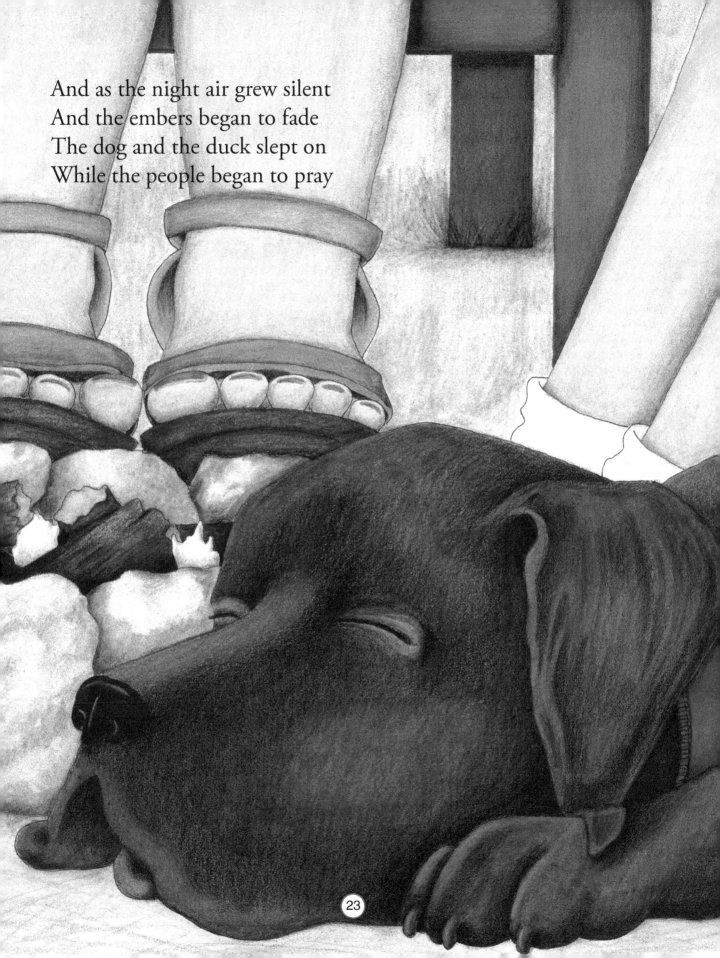

And as the night air grew silent
And the embers began to fade
The dog and the duck slept on
While the people began to pray

23

They thanked God for His creation
For the gift of freedom from sin
They thanked him for Jesus Christ
And the Holy Spirit within

They thanked God for the love of family
For the fellowship of good friends
For a giant dog and a little duck
On whom they could depend

25

Depend on to make them laugh
To entertain them for hours and hours
An odd pair that, when combined,
Were like a beautiful bouquet of flowers

Yes, a dog and his duck
Though unlikely friends
Were the best of buddies
Until the very end—

And if heaven welcomes animals
You can be sure that you will find
Bo Bear and Duck Duck
Side by side…all of the time

About the Author

Shelley Jukanovich began writing at the age of eleven. After receiving her Bachelor of Arts in Tourism, her love of writing led her to further her education by attending *the Institute of Children's Literature.* She earned a diploma in 'Writing for Children and Teenagers.' Shelley spent several years writing for magazines prior to taking a job in education. She was inspired to write a children's book after observing the unique and playful friendship between her dog, Bo, and her pet duck. This is her first children's book. She strives to bring joy and hope to her readers by sharing real-life testimonies and stories that inspire. Shelley loves to travel and has lived abroad teaching English as a Foreign Language. She also enjoys reading, hunting for agates, paddle boarding and spending time with her family and friends. She is thankful for her local church where she serves as a leader in both Women's Ministries and small groups. Shelley lives on a quaint island in the Northwest with her husband and three teenagers.

sjukanovich@gmail.com

About the Illustrator

J aime Wickstrom's favorite activity as a child was to create art at the kitchen table with crisp white paper, pencils, colorful markers and a fresh pan of watercolor paints. She's delighted to admit that it's still her favorite activity today, although she now works at a desk and has accumulated a few more art supplies because she believes you can never have too many! She often draws with a smile on her face and hopes that her winsome illustrations of people and animals enjoying life will bring cheer to whoever sees them.

Jaime still lives on the charming little island where she grew up, is married to her highschool sweetheart Eric, has two pretty awesome kids, and spends her days drawing, painting and praising the Lord. Anytime you need a reason to smile, visit her website and social media pages.

www.jaimewickstrom.com
FB: jaimewickstromstudioart
Instagram: @jaimewickstromstudioart

Lightning Source UK Ltd.
Milton Keynes UK
UKHW050354280619
345159UK00001B/6/P